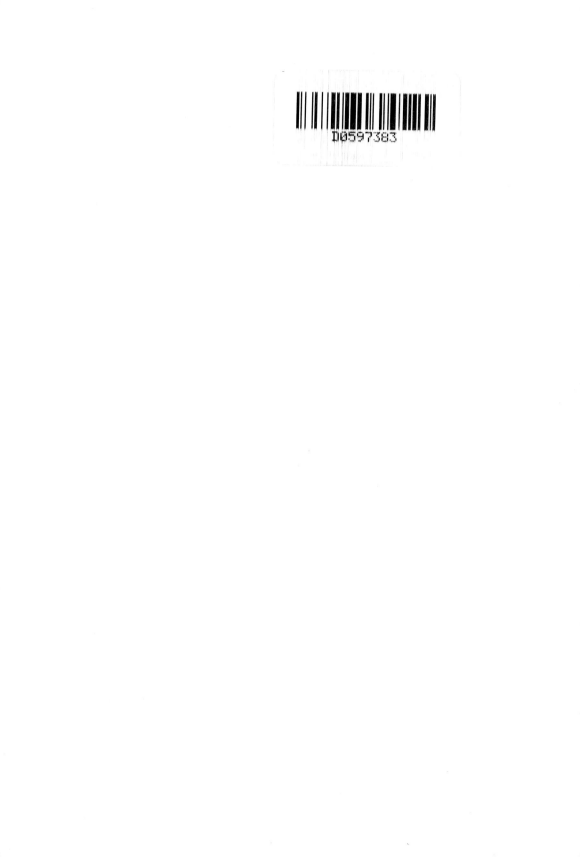

D0597383

JAN K.OSTROWSKI, JANUSZ PODLECKI
WAWEL
CASTLE AND CATHEDRAL

WAWEL
CASTLE AND CATHEDRAL

Text:
© JAN K. OSTROWSKI

Photographs:
© JANUSZ PODLECKI

PUBLISHING HOUSE „KARPATY" – ANDRZEJ ŁĄCZYŃSKI
CRACOW 1999

Design:
© MAGDALENA MICHALSKA

Editor:
BARBARA ROBAK

Photographs and computer processing:
© JANUSZ PODLECKI

Translated into English
by © JADWIGA PIĄTKOWSKA

Second published

ISBN 83-85204-70-9

WYDAWNICTWO „KARPATY" – ANDRZEJ ŁĄCZYŃSKI
30-074 Kraków, ul. Kazimierza Wielkiego 21, tel./fax (48-12) 634-31-05

WAWEL,

a limestone hill which commands Cracow, has been as much important for the urban and social structure of the city as the Acropolis in Athens, the Capitol in Rome or the Kremlin in Moscow, as the historic seat of the spiritual and temporal power. For the Poles it performs yet another function: it serves as the symbol of national unity and tradition.

* *

*

The five-hectar area of the hill contains a vast complex of historic buildings which once operated as a semi-autonomous town. Yet the historic and artistic value of Wawel is best represented by the Royal Castle and the Cathedral.

The Vistula near the Norbertine
Convent, Wawel in the background.

Wawel Castle from the south-west,
with the Sandomierska Tower (left)
and the Senator's Tower (Lubranka). →

The Thieves' Tower.

A view of Wawel Hill
from the south-west.

A view of Wawel Hill
from the north-west.

The Heraldic Gate.

A view of the Castle
from the north-east. ↗

A section of the late-eighteenth-
-century fortifications.

THE CASTLE

on Wawel Hill served as the seat of the kings of Poland from the mid-eleventh century to the early seventeenth century. Defensive structures together with the royal residence occupied the east part of the hill, which is confirmed by the oldest records. The pre-Romanesque and Romanesque buildings are represented by the remains of the *palatium* preserved under the north wing of the present Castle. The *palatium* consisted of a large hall (the twenty-four-pillar hall), a dwelling tower and St. Gereon's Church. Nearby was a square stone building, probably a storehouse, and the Rotunda of the Virgin Mary (also known as the Church of SS. Felix and Adauctus).

In the fourteenth and fifteenth centuries a Gothic castle, comparable in size with the present one, was gradually constructed around a quadrangle. First, probably at the turn of the thirteenth and fourteenth centuries, a defensive stone tower containing living quarters was built in the north-east of the hill; it was later called the Hen's Foot Tower. Then another tower was added, which was called the Danish Tower from the fifteenth century onward, as Eric, King of Denmark, lived there during his stay in Cracow. Both towers, refashioned in the second half of the fourteenth century, contained state apartments. We can still admire vaulted Gothic chambers on their ground floors, and outside, the slender oriel of the Hen's Foot Tower and the fine masonry facing on the Danish Tower.

In 1499 the Gothic Castle was consumed by fire and its reconstruction followed a different line. A new magnificent residence was required as the old castle could no longer meet the needs of the Jagiellon dynasty which ruled most of Central and Eastern Europe (in Poland and Lithuania as well as in Hungary and Bohemia) and aspired after the Imperial Crown. The Castle was restored and expanded between 1504 and 1535, in the reigns of King Alexander (1501–1506) and Sigismund the Elder (1506–1548). The works were begun in the west wing, next to the Cathedral, which was completed in the years 1504–1507 as King Alexander's palace. It was built mainly by Eberhard Rosemberger, a Cracow mason born in Koblenz. He was responsible for masonry works, while the stonework, obviously regarded as a separate task, was the responsibility of an Italian, Francesco of Florence, who executed window-surrounds and the fine oriel on the second floor. Thus new Renaissance Italian art was first introduced into monumental architecture in Poland.

The west wing was initially designed as a separate rectangular three-storey building covered with a steep Gothic roof. Each storey contained several large rooms in single-file arrangement. According to Central European tradition, and contrary to Italian custom, the ground floor held service rooms, the first floor – private apartments, and the second floor – state apartments.

In the years 1507–1516 the north wing was erected according to the same plan, thus connecting King Alexander's palace with the Gothic buildings in the north-east corner. Hence functional factors demanded that the vast construction, which retained the single-file room arrangement, be fitted with cloisters as the necessary communication gallery. So practical requirements resulted in the most splendid and most typically Renaissance element of the Wawel Castle architecture, as Francesco of Florence adopted the model popular in Florentine buildings: two storeys of arcaded loggias and the straight-line-topped upper storey. In 1521–1529, after Francesco's death, the east wing was built by the master-mason Benedykt, a local man of German descent, and in 1530–1536 the south

The Arcade Court, the west and north wings.

The Royal Castle and the Cathedral from the air.

wing was added. The arcades at those two wings, modelled on the ones constructed by Francesco of Florence yet with some minor improvements, are the work of the eminent Florentine architect and sculptor in the royal service, Bartolomeo Berrecci.

Wawel Castle is a multi-wing complex with an inner court in the shape of an irregular pentagon. The palace proper consists of the west, north and east wings. The south end of the west wing is taken by the building of the former royal kitchen, which does not have arcaded loggias, and the south wing is a screen-wall with arcades added. The form of the structure is a compromise between the local Gothic building tradition and the Italian Renaissance model. Late-Gothic elements include the spacial plan of the palace and its slender proportions emphasised by the high steep roofs. Italian motifs comprise some of the masonry (window-surrounds, portals) and particularly the arcaded loggias which encircle the court. The latter were obviously the builder's response to functional needs, but their form was derived from fifteenth-century Florentine architecture, although the specific features of the site enforced some particular solutions. Italian courts are smaller than the Wawel court, yet they are generally strictly regular, while this is not the case in Cracow. Also, the greater hight of the second floor (*piano nobile*) and straight-line eaves instead of arcades resulted in the extremely elongated columns of the upper storey. Master Francesco solved the problem by resorting to a device used in Gothic architecture: he clasped the column shafts in the middle with decorative stone rings. Further up, above the capitals, he inserted urn-shaped extensions to disperse the deep shadows in which the broad eaves engulfed the capitals. In the sixteenth century architectural elements were painted in bright colours and the roof was also decorated with multi-coloured

The Castle-keeper's lodgings on the ground floor, Room I.

The Castle-keeper's lodgings on the ground floor, Room III. →

↙ The Castle-keeper's lodgings on the ground floor, Room II.

The landing of the Envoys' Stairs on the first floor, with a Flemish arras tapestry ca 1580, showing a deer hunt.

The first room of the living apartment on the first floor.

The second room of the living apartment on the first floor.

The third room of the living apartment on the first floor.

glazed tiles. Under the eaves ran a colourful frieze with the busts of Roman emperors, now only partly preserved.

The interiors of the Renaissance residence of King Sigismund the Elder were generally decorated in a uniform way. The rooms were covered with painted timber or coffer ceilings. Underneath ran painted friezes: their subjects gave names to the rooms (the Tournament Room, the Troops Parade Room etc.). Among those who painted the friezes was Hans Dürer, brother of the famous Albrecht. The recent restoration of the paintings in the Tournament Room revealed considerable stylistic differences in particular sections, which allowed for making conjectures as to Dürer's authorship of some specific parts of the frieze. The walls beneath the frieze were covered with suitable hangings or remained clear, providing space for pictures and especially for arras tapestries. The rooms were furnished with colourful stoves and with doorways, which in the east wing were of specific Gothic and Renaissance character. The most unique decoration was once the coffer ceiling of the Envoys' Room which contained 194 carved and painted timber human heads, the work of Sebastian Tauerbach and Jan Janda. The date of the ceiling and the heads is not certain because of the fire which destroyed this part of the Castle in 1536, but it is generally assumed to be 1535–1540. The origin and symbolism of the heads are not clear and have been long disputed. It is certain, however, that the 30 heads which have been preserved have been placed incorrectly in the inappropriately restored ceiling.

The decoration of the Wawel interiors was defined by the set of ideas which cannot be fully decoded today. It consisted mainly of frieze presentations and inscriptions which alluded to both

The bedroom in the living apartment on the first floor.

The Grey Passageway on the first floor.

Christian and ancient tradition, mainly the stoic one. The maxims carved on the doorways are typically stoic, as VELIS QUOD POSSIS or MODERATA DURANT. Of a similar character is the frieze in the Envoys' Room, most interesting from the iconographic point of view, which presents the way of human life according to the treatise of the ancient philosopher Cebes. The obscure details notwithstanding, the Castle interiors proclaimed the glory and virtue of the ruler, who was severe to the enemies and forbearing to the subjects, wise and pious.

Historical documents bear witness to the amazing splendour of the residence of the last Jagiellon kings. Unfortunately, its only survivor are the Flemish arras tapestries commissioned by Sigismund Augustus (1548–1572) in the best workshops of Brussels in the years 1550–1571. The tapestries were made by a labour-consuming method of coloured woollen thread interwoven with gold and silver. The collection consisted originally of about 400 items, of which 136 have survived. The Wawel tapestries contain three groups. One, most monumental, presents biblical scenes (the Paradise, Noah's story, the building of the Tower of Babel), executed after the designs of the 'Flemish Raphael', Michiel van Coxcie. The second are verdures: usually smaller tapestries showing landscapes and real or fantastic animals. The third group consists of heraldic tapestries bearing the king's arms and initials framed with elaborate grotesque motifs. There are also small tapestries which were to be hung above doorways or to serve for upholstery. The tapestries were made to order, to fit particular rooms in the Castle.

The major architectonic element of Wawel Castle date back to the first half of the sixteenth century, yet some of its interiors were fashioned later. In 1595 the north wing and some of the east wing were consumed by two successive fires. In the years 1599–1603 King Sigismund III commissioned the restoration, or more precisely, the reconstruction of that part of the Castle, in the early--Baroque style, which is known in Poland as the Vasa style. The works were supervised by the royal

The bedroom of President Ignacy Mościcki.

The interior of the oriel in the Hen's Foot Tower.

A cabinet on the first floor of Sigusmund III' Tower, showing the vaulted ceiling.

The Tournament Room.

A Florentine dowry chest (*cassone*), ca 1450.

The Troops Parade Room with the sixteenth-century arras tapestries decorated with the initials of King Sigismund Augustus.

The Envoys' Room. →

A detail of the frieze in the Troops Parade Room.

architect, Giovanni Trevano, who erected two modest towers in the corners of the north wing and built a new large staircase, known as the Senators' Stairs, at the junction of the north and west wings. Contrary to the narrow and steep Envoys' Stairs from the first half of the sixteenth century, the Senators' Stairs, wide and comfortable, divided into flights at landings, were perfectly suited for Baroque state occasions. The interiors which Trevano refashioned were given new stonework made of the brown marble from the Kielce region. Its highest achievement is the magnificent fireplace in the Bird Room. The ceilings in some of the rooms were given stucco ornaments, other rooms received timber ceilings which, however, differed from the Renaissance ones as they consisted of gilded frames containing paintings. Unfortunately, little of the original decoration of Sigismund III's apartments has survived: only stonework and some stuccoes, while everything else is the result of restoration works. The walls are covered with eighteenth-century cordovan, that is an equivalent of wallpaper made of soft printed and painted leather. The ceilings were reconstructed after the original ceilings in the castle at Podhorce and filled in with modern paintings by eminent Polish painters of the 1930s.

An arras from the Sigismund Augustus collection, with animals and a landscape.

Marcin Kober, Portrait of Queen Anne, daughter of King Sigismund the Elder, after 1586. ↘

A section of the ceiling in the Envoys' Room.

Portrait of King Sigismund the Elder, ca 1540.

The Zodiac Room.

The Planets Room, with the painting *Entering Noah's Ark* by Leonardo Bassano.

In 1609 King Sigismund III took permanent residence in Warsaw, so Wawel was *de facto* deprived of its function as a royal seat, and consequently its gradual decline began. In 1655–1657 it was seriously damaged by the Swedes, and the second Swedish occupation in 1702 was particularly disastrous. The fire started by the soldiers, the most serious in the Castle's history, destroyed a major part of the original Renaissance decorations, including the magnificent stoves. The damaged parts were only provisionally protected, and the single eighteenth-century addition to the Castle architecture was a state room on the first floor, furnished for the visit to Cracow paid by King Stanislas Augustus Poniatowski in 1787. The occupation of Wawel by the Prussians, who in 1795 plundered the crown treasury, and then appropriation of Cracow by Austria began the worst period in the Castle's history.

For most of the nineteenth century the old royal Castle served as barracks for the Austrian army, which resulted in further damage to its unique architecture and decoration. Gradually smaller historic structures on the hill disappeared, including the medieval churches of St. Michael and St. George. In the mid-nineteenth century the whole of Wawel was included into a system of fortifications, and along its south-west limit the heavy buildings of the army hospital were erected. Twice, in 1830 and 1882, a restoration of the royal residence was planned, and designs were prepared by the architects Franciszek Maria Lanci and Tomasz Pryliński respectively.

In 1905, following the repeated petitions by the Poles, the Emperor Francis Joseph gave his permission for the army to evacuate the Castle. Wawel was declared to become an official imperial residence, but it was clear that it was to function as the most important Polish historical monument. The restoration works were first supervised by Zygmunt Hendel and then by Adolf Szyszko-Bohusz. Restoration was accompanied by architectonic and archaeological research, which made it possible to reconstruct the successive phases of the Castle construction. The most famous find was the pre-Romanesque Rotunda of the Virgin Mary which was discovered within the walls of the royal kitchen.

Tommaso Dolabella (?), *Battle of Lepanto*, after 1632, a detail.

The Bird Room.

The chapel on the second floor.

Portrait of Janusz Radziwiłł, late seventeenth century.

The Dutch Cabinet in Sigismund III' Tower.

Workshop of Peter Paul Rubens, Portrait
of Prince Ladislaus Sigismund
(later King Ladislaus IV), 1624.

The equestrian portrait of Prince Ladislaus Sigismund (later King Ladislaus IV), after 1624 ☆
Szymon Boguszowicz (?), Portrait of Maryna Mniszech as Tzarina of Muscovy, ca 1606.
The Eagle Room, with a seventeenth-century tapestry
showing *The Death of Decius Mus*, after P. P. Rubens.

The works were continued during the First World War and after Poland regained independence in 1918. Seen from today's perspective, those works deserve great credit for their scope and quality.

The return of many historical items by Soviet Russia after the Treaty of Riga in 1921 provided a major part of the of the inventory of the museum into which the Castle was to be transformed. Its most precious jewels were the tapestries of King Sigismund Augustus. Historic items were also obtained by purchase and by numerous bequests and deposits. Most important among them were the legacies by Count Leon Piniński and Count Jerzy Mycielski which formed the core of the Wawel painting collection before 1939. In 1930 the Wawel Museum was formally instituted as a branch of the State Art Collections. Simultaneously, the Castle served as the official residence of the President of Poland.

At the very beginning of the Second World War the greatest treasures of the Wawel Museum were sent to Canada, yet most items remained in the Castle, which was turned into the seat of the occupation authorities of the General Gouvernement and the residence of Governor Hans Frank. It was beneficial in a way as the historic places and items were protected from systematic destruction practised in Warsaw. However, the years of the Nazi occupation brought the unfortunate reconstruction of the royal kitchen and of a wing of the Austrian hospital in the architectural style adopted by the Third Reich.

Immediately after liberation from the Nazis work was resumed by the Management of the Restoration of the Royal Castle and by the State Art Collections. The Museum, although much impoverished, opened its doors to the public. In 1953 Professor Jerzy Szablowski was nominated Museum Director; he was chiefly responsible for its thorough modernisation. After the mid-1950s historical

Henri Gascar, Family portrait of John III Sobieski, 1691.

The Senators' Room with the arras tapestries from the Sigismund Augustus collection showing Noah's story.

The tapestry *Noah's Drunkenness* from the Sigismund Augustus collection.

A seventeenth-century Turkish tent.

The Exhibition of Oriental Art, the Weapons Room.

The Exhibition of Oriental Art, Ceramics Room above the gate designed by Berrecci.

The Crown Treasury, a seventeenth-century Polish saddle and trappings. →

The Crown Treasury, the King Casimir Room on the ground floor of the Hen's Foot Tower.

and archaeological research works were intensified, as part of the programme to celebrate the millennium of the Polish State. In the years 1959–1961 the treasures which had been sent to Canada at the beginning of the war were restored to Wawel, among them the famous arras tapestries. The exhibitions which were opened soon afterwards marked the high point in the Museum history and included the Crown Treasury, Armoury and the unique Exhibition of Oriental Tents.

The Royal Castle at Wawel is a museum and a historical residence, which consists of several special sections. In its main part, the royal apartments, the royal residence was restored, as it might have been in the sixteenth and early seventeenth centuries. The finest among the exhibits is the arras collection of Sigismund Augustus. Of high artistic merit are also the Italian Renaissance furniture and old portraits, mainly of the royal sitters. The restored Crown Treasury occupies the Gothic rooms on the ground floor of the Hen's Foot Tower and the Danish Tower. It contains items which belonged to Polish kings as well as gold- and silverwork, fine armour and caparisons. Next to it is the Armoury, which was assembled mainly in the post-war period, owing to the acquisition of the collection of the eminent arms collector, Bruno Konczakowski of Cieszyn. The east wing of the Castle holds the exhibition of the art of the Near and Far East which displays textiles, ceramics, weapons and other metalwork. The glory of the collection are seven seventeenth-century Turkish tents. The condition of most of them is, however, very poor, so they are being subjected to complex conservation procedures. The ground floor of the former royal kitchen houses the Lost Wawel Exhibition which consists of an archaeological site presenting the Castle historic architecture and exhibits found during excavation and restoration works.

As all museums, the Royal Castle at Wawel aims at expanding its collections, although it is difficult to acquire items suitable for a royal residence. Therefore of immense importance is the generous gift bequeathed in 1994 by Professor Karolina Lanckorońska, the last surviving member of a great historic family. The legacy consists of over 80 pictures, mainly by Italian Renaissance painters, from the family collection of the Counts Lanckoroński. The collection requires extensive conservation works, but a number of paintings have been restored and are now displayed in the Castle rooms.

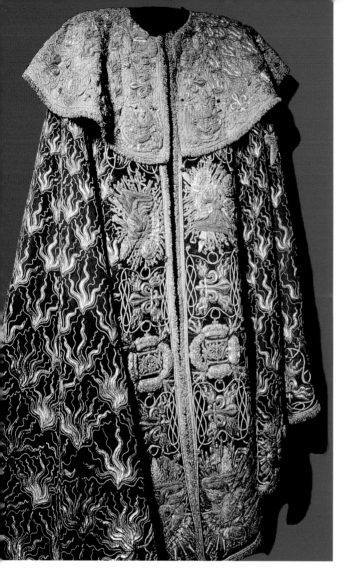

The Crown Treasury, the robe of the Order of the Holy Spirit which belonged to King John III Sobieski.

The Crown Treasury, the "Szczerbiec" Sword. ↗

The Crown Treasury, the sword and the hat presented by the Pope to King John III Sobieski.

The Armoury, cannon and lance-type weapons in the basement of the Hen's Foot Tower.

The Armoury, seventeenth- and eighteenth-century armour.

A room in the Senators' Tower.

A stove tile, by Bartosz of Kazimierz, first quarter of the sixteenth century.
"The Lost Wawel" archaeological site, with a fragment of the Rotunda of SS. Felix and Adauctus.

The model of Wawel Hill showing the site as it was in the eighteenth century.

THE CATHEDRAL.

At the meeting of King Boleslaus the Brave with the Emperor Otto III in 1000 it was decided to constitute the Polish church metropolis. One of the sees founded at that time was located in Cracow and the site for a cathedral was chosen, which was the origin of this principal church of the city of Cracow. The first cathedral at Wawel, built around 1025, was pre-Romanesque in style. We can partly decipher its shape owing to its remains in the basement. The second cathedral, founded by Duke Ladislaus I Herman, was built ca 1090–1142. It was a large Romanesque basilica, with a nave and two aisles, constructed of limestone ashlars, with two choirs (in the east and the west end) and probably with two towers. The character and scope of its architecture can be conjectured from the lower part of the Curate Tower (the Silver Bells Tower), and particularly from St. Leonard's Crypt, which was situated under the old west choir. The style of the remains points to Western Europe, to the areas on the Rhein and the Mosa, as the source of inspiration for the architecture of the cathedral built by Duke Herman.

After the Romanesque cathedral had been burnt in 1305, Bishop Nanker began the construction of a new Gothic church in 1320. In 1346 the presbytery was completed, and in 1364 the main body of the church with the transept. The picturesque and erratic mass of the present Cathedral has retained the bold structure of the Gothic church, in spite of numerous subsequent extensions and alterations. It was built on the plan of a cross formed by the juncture of the nave and the presbytery with the transept. The body of the church is that of a basilica, with the nave and two aisles, and the rectangular presbytery is encompassed by the ambulatory. On the church axis, at the east part of the ambulatory, is the Lady Chapel, larger than other chapels. The Gothic character of the Cathedral is more evident at the west end, where the west front has retained the stonework of the nave almost intact, flanked by two fifteenth-century chapels, the Holy Trinity Chapel and the Holy Cross Chapel. From the south the medieval body of the church has been obscured by the numerous later extensions which form a unique stylistic mixture.

Wawel Cathedral defined the development trends of church architecture in Cracow in the fourteenth century, but its interior is different in some ways from other town churches. The interior has gained more space with the introduction of the transept and more sophistication with the fine stone facing. Yet many later parish and monastic churches in Cracow and Kazimierz are of greater size and more impressive hight.

The best preserved part of the medieval Cathedral is the Holy Cross Chapel, founded in the second half of the fifteenth century as the burial place of King Casimir IV Jagiellon and his wife, Queen Elizabeth of Austria. It is a small rectangular structure, its exterior decorated with elegant stone fluting. Its interior is almost entirely covered with Byzantine wall-paintings, the work of Ruthenian artists who were often employed by the early Jagiellon kings brought up in the Orthodox tradition and culture. The hieratic, spiritual figures of Orthodox saints are juxtaposed to the paintings and sculptures of two triptychs: of the Holy Trinity and Our Lady of Pity, which date back to the 1450s and 1460s respectively, and show the features of late-Gothic realism and expression. In a chapel corner is the magnificent tomb of King Casimir IV carved by Wit Stwosz (Veit Stoss). The burial place of Elizabeth, the mother of kings of Poland, Hungary and Bohemia, is marked only by a simple slab in the floor. The uniform style of the chapel is disturbed, however, by the huge eighteenth-century monument to Bishop Kajetan Sołtyk.

After the unification of the country and the coronation of Ladislaus the Short in the early fourteenth century, Cracow Cathedral received the status of the chief royal church. Almost all coronations and burials of Polish kings took place there. The Cathedral boasts an impressive array of royal

A view of the Cathedral
from the south-west. →

A view of the Sigismund Chapel from the south.

The Cathedral west front.

The Cathedral interior with the Shrine of St. Stanislaus.

The sarcophagus of St. Stanislaus, by Peter von der Rennen, 1661–1671.

Antoni Madeyski, the tomb of King Ladislaus III, 1906. ↘

The effigy of King Ladislaus Jagiełło on the sarcophagus, second quarter of the fifteenth century.

HOC OPVS FEDERICO CARDINALI CAZIMIRI FILIO, CVI ·QVINQVE·
ET · TRIGINTA ANNIS · EXACTIS · M.D.III. MARCII · XIII · OBIECERAT ·
CARISSIMO DIVVS SIGISMVNDVS · REX · POLONIAE · PIENTISSIMVS
POSVIT · AB · INCARNATIONE · DOMINI · M.D.X. ·

The tomb of Cardinal Frederic Jagiellon, 1510.

Wit Stwosz (Veit Stoss), the tomb of Casimir IV Jagiellon, 1492–1494 ☆
Wit Stwosz, the effigy of King Casimir IV on the sarcophagus.

tombs and monuments. The earliest of them is the tomb of Ladislaus the Short carved in sandstone in the first half of the fourteenth century, placed in the arcade which joins the presbytery with the north wing of the ambulatory. The supine effigy of the king lies on the massive sarcophagus. The sculpture, probably made after his death, attempts nevertheless to capture his likeness as the face is far from the ideal type, with bushy Slav whiskers. The side walls of the sarcophagus feature the figures of mourners who symbolise the grief of the subjects after the death of the ruler. The canopy above is neo-Gothic, made in 1900–1903.

The Cracow royal tomb reached its classical form in the monument of Casimir the Great dating from 1370–1382. It continues and further develops the concept inherent in the tomb of Lasislaus the Short, indicating as well the influence of the Viennese court art. It is placed symmetrically in relation to the earlier tomb, to the south of the presbytery. It was made of red Hungarian marble, which adds to its royal magnificence. The tomb-chest with the supine effigy of the king is surmounted by the canopy which rests on six slender columns. This motif, modelled most certainly on the papal monuments in Avignion, bears a deep and appealing message as it signifies the dome of heaven above the late king.

The tomb of Ladislaus Jagiełło has been much discussed as far as its date and artistic models are concerned. Such details apart, it is an outstanding example of the international Gothic style popular in the second quarter of the fifteenth century which also continues the tradition of the monuments of the last Piast kings. Jagiełło is presented as the knight-king, conqueror of evil which is symbolised as a dragon at his feet, as a mighty ruler, which is indicated by the arms of his lands, but also as the king beloved by his subjects, which is conveyed by the mourners with very Polish faces who are holding the heraldic arms. The canopy, which was begun at the same time as the tomb, was completed as late as 1519–1524 in the Renaissance style.

The development cycle of the royal tomb-chest culminates in the tomb of Casimir IV Jagiellon, signed by Wit Stwosz and dated 1492. The sculptor's assistant was Jorg Huber who carved the

The interior of the Vasa Chapel, ca 1664–1676 ☆ The gate to the Vasa Chapel, by Michał Weinhold, 1673.

The interior of the Sigismund Chapel, with the monuments of King Sigismund the Elder and King Sigismund Augustus, 1529–1531 and 1574–1575; on the left the monument of Queen Anne, 1571–1575.

The Silver Altar in the Sigismund Chapel, 1531–1538. →

Antoni Madeyski, the tomb of Queen Jadwiga, 1902.

Francesco of Florence, the tomb of King John Albert, 1502–1505.

capitals of the canopy. The design of the monument resembles the earlier royal tombs, yet it is unique in its expression and dynamism. The king, dressed in liturgical robes, seems to writhe in death agony, the mourners manifest their grief by dramatic gestures, even the architectonic elements of the canopy and the tracery on the sarcophagus are convulsively twisted. These dramatic artistic means express a complex iconographic message of eschatological character.

In 1501, less than ten years after Casimir's death, died prematurely his son and successor, John Albert. By the end of that year Francesco of Florence, the artist commissioned to make his tomb, arrived in Cracow. He has been already mentioned as one of the chief architects who worked on the reconstruction and extension of the Castle. However, as carving the figure of the late king was not among his skills, the task was given to a local artist. The tombstone continues the tradition of the earlier royal monuments, yet its artistic effect is of a lower order. Francesco, however, demonstrated his skills and his command of new art in the architectonic setting of the tomb. He gave up the idea of a free-standing monument and according to Florentine custom placed the tomb in a large niche which is composed of purely Renaissance architectonic elements. He abandoned the local traditional tomb type and introduced a revolutionary stylistic novelty, yet he was careful to emphasise the appropriate message. The ornaments in the niche stress (perhaps in a rather exaggerated manner) John Albert's role as a knight and benefactor of the country, while the arcade above the king's effigy is a modern version of the canopy which is synonymous with heaven.

Some dozen years after the completion of John Albert's tomb, construction works started on the burial chapel of the last Jagiellon kings, the finest jewel of Renaissance art in Poland. The idea of such a chapel was conceived by King Sigismund the Elder after the death of his first wife, Barbara Zapolya, in 1515. The task was commissioned to Bartolomeo Berrecci, who presented his design to the king in 1517. Construction works started in 1519 and the chapel was consecrated in 1533. Berrecci's work in Wawel Cathedral is the purest example of Italian Renaissance architecture outside Italy. Its architectonic and decorative design goes back to the best Tuscan models of the turn of

The tomb of King Casimir the Great, ca 1370–1382 ☆ The tomb of King Ladislaus the Short, second quarter of the fourteenth century.

Santi Gucci, a detail of the monument of King Steven Bathory, 1595.

The Lady Chapel with the monument of King Steven Bathory, Santi Gucci, 1595. →

Jan Michałowicz, the tomb of Bishop Filip Padniewski, ca 1575. ↘

Bartolomeo Berrecci, the tomb of Bishop Piotr Tomicki, 1532–1535.

The Cathedral Treasury, the cross made of ducal diadems, ca 1250 and 1472–1488 ☆
The Cathedral Treasury, St. Maurice's spear, presented by the Emperor Otto III to King Boleslaus the Brave in 1000.

the fifteenth and sixteenth centuries; Leonardo da Vinci's theoretical designs must have exerted some influence as well. According to the Renaissance principle which extols the perfection of the central form, the chapel is built on a square plan. It has the shape of a cube topped with the octagonal drum which supports the elongated dome. The slender, almost steeple-like proportions of the structure were conditioned by the need to adjust it to the Gothic character of the background. The soaring dome, gilded in the late sixteenth century, is the cynosure of the south front of the Cathedral. The chapel interior is bedecked with grotesque decorations which, however, do not blur its clear architectonic proportions. The wall decoration is based on the triumphal arch, and niches in the walls display figures of saints. Above, high up on the ceiling of the lantern, the builder's signature has been placed: BARTHOLO FLORENTINO OPIFICE. Thus Barrecci's part in creating the architecture of the chapel and outlining its sculpture decorations is undisputed. Yet the authors of particular carved figures and reliefs have not been identified, although we know a dozen or so names of the sculptors who, according to the sources, worked in Berrecci's workshop. It must be noted that if the stonework in the chapel is by Italian artists, the bronze and silverwork was commissioned in Nuremberg. The fine silver altar is by Georg Pencz, Melchior Baier and Peter Flötner.

The royal monument, carved of red Hungarian marble, has been modelled on the tomb of John Albert. Its present appearance is the result of the alterations made in the years 1574–1575 when the niche was split in half and the sarcophagus with King Sigismund the Elder's effigy was raised, to make room for the parallel effigy of King Sigismund Augustus. Santi Gucci, who was the author of the alterations, carved also the relief on the front surface of the royal pew, with the figure of Queen Anne, daughter of King Sigismund the Elder and wife of King Steven Bathory.

King Sigismund the Elder erected his mausoleum to commemorate himself and his family. In his design the durability of the chapel stonework was to be matched by the continuing regular religious service held in the chapel, particularly by liturgical singing. According to Renaissance custom, based on neo-Platonic tradition, the monument presented the king in sleep. The motif of the triumphal arch, the dome functioning as a canopy, the Latin inscriptions, the heraldic arms and portraits of King Sigismund which portray him as Alexander the Great and Solomon, all this presents the ideal monument of the monarch. In spite of the obvious classical references, the message has been conveyed by the Christian symbolic language, which concurs with the sacral character of the place.

The decoration of the upper parts of the chapel is of a different order, its main motifs being mythological scenes in which sea-monsters with fish-tails play (or perhaps fight) with naked nymphs. We can also identify Daphne, Cleopatra and Hercules. The meaning of these decorations, quite surprising in a Christian church, has been debated by eminent Polish art historians for over twenty five years. Some interpret it as the creative initiative of Berrecci taken without the King's leave; as a humanist, he placed his name in the lantern, above the dome which symbolises heaven, and thus expressed his belief in the artist's divine creativity. Some other art historians attempt to reconcile the message in the two parts of the chapel, on the principle of the syncretic ideas of humanism which aimed at integrating classical tradition and Christian culture. The latter art historians point to the eschatological aspects of the nereids and the vanitarian symbolism of sphinxes, griffins, eagles and dolphins. The most recent hypothesis identifies the creatures with tails as giants and the scene as a gigantomachia, that is the classical allegory of the struggle of good and evil. The presentations seems to refer to the situation in Poland, in particular to King Sigismund the Elder's firm stand against the Reformation.

The Cathedral was also the burial place of the Bishops of Cracow, many of whom commissioned their burial chapels. The Renaissance chapel of Bishop Piotr Tomicki was built by Bartolomeo Berrecci about 1530. Its architectonic design, much more modest than in the Sigismund Chapel,

The Cathedral Treasury, a fourteenth-century crown ☆ The Cathedral Treasury, the mitre of Bishop Tomasz Strzempiński, 1455–1460 and 1523–1535.

The Cathedral Treasury, the stirrup which belonged to Grand Vizier Kara Mustafa, one of the trophies captured by King John III Sobieski at the battle of Vienna, 1683.
The Cathedral Treasury, the reliquary for St. Stanislaus' head, by Marcin Marciniec, 1504 ☆
☆ The Cathedral Treasury, the chasuble donated by Piotr Kmita, 1504.

The Cathedral Treasury, replicas of King Casimir the Great's regalia from his tomb.

was widely imitated all over Poland. It contains a fine monument of the humanist bishop. Of a later date are the chapels founded by the Bishops: Samuel Maciejowski (ca mid-sixteenth century), Andrzej Zebrzydowski (1562–1563) and Filip Padniewski (1572–1575). The latter two are the work of the first eminent Renaissance artist of Polish descent, Jan Michałowicz.

Mannerism is best represented among the Cathedral monuments by the memorial to King Steven Bathory which was commissioned by his wife, Queen Anne. This work of 1595 by Santi Gucci, placed in the Lady Chapel, generally continues the Renaissance tradition of royal tombs, but is different in its mannerist flat treatment as well as in decorative and imaginative ornament.

In the seventeenth and eighteenth centuries many new elements were added to the Cathedral. The proportions of the entire structure were changed by raising the ambulatory. On the main axis of the interior new elements appeared which represent a new artistic and ideological message: the shrine of St. Stanislaus (1628–1630), in the form of an open-work chapel topped with a dome, and the High Altar (1648–1649). Next to the Sigismund Chapel the Vasa Chapel was erected as its twin copy. The similarity was obviously intended. The kings of the Vasa dynasty, who were elected in free elections, had also hereditary claims to the throne owing to their family links with the Jagiellonian dynasty. This relationship was to be emphasised by commissioning a family mausoleum in the Cathedral, closely modelled on the memorial chapel of the last Jagiellon kings. The history of the Vasa Chapel is long and complex. Its erection was first suggested in the will of King Sigismund III in 1598, yet the construction started only towards the end of the reign of King John II Casimir in 1664. When the king abdicated and left Poland, the chapel was completed by Bishop Andrzej Trzebicki in 1676. Architecture was not destined to play any role in the political propaganda of the Vasa kings, as at the chapel's completion none of them was alive. Contrary to the exterior which follows the Renaissance model, the interior was designed in the Baroque style which emphasises the austerity of the Counter-reformation. Most architectonic elements are of black marble, which contrasts sharply with the white and gold carved figures and ornament. Unfortunately, the name of the author of the Vasa mausoleum has remained unknown. The only feeble clue we have is the fact that Giovanni Battista Gisleni participated in the arrangement of the royal crypts after the death of King Ladislaus IV. Thus that eminent architect might have also designed the chapel, for its interior seems to correspond to his own style.

The Vasa Chapel was the last royal mausoleum built within the Cathedral. The introduction of elective monarchy as well as transferring the royal court to Warsaw did not encourage similar ventures. The memorials to later rulers were erected long after their death, and some were not commemorated at all. The memorials to King John III Sobieski and Queen Marie-Casimire and to King Michael Wiśniowiecki and Queen Eleonora were placed next to each other in the ambulatory as late as 1753–1760 owing to the funds raised by Michał Kazimierz Radziwiłł. They were designed by the architect Francesco Placidi and carved by Mrowiński. Both memorials are typical of the late Baroque, of allegorical character, featuring personifications of royal virtues and figures of Turkish captives.

The Baroque style is also represented by the chapels built by Bishop Jakub Zadzik (1645–1650) and Bishops Andrzej and Jan Lipski (erected ca 1634 and rebuilt in expressive form by Placidi in 1743–1746). Some bishops were commemorated not by chapels but by memorials placed on the transept pillars. Thus around the shrine of St. Stanislaus a Baroque complex was created which combined the intricate composition with the theological concept of permanent adoration of the martyred bishop by his successors in the Cracow see. The finest of them is the memorial to Bishop Piotr Gębicki, made in 1657 by the architect Giovanni Battista Gisleni and the sculptor Francesco de Rossi.

St. Leonard's Crypt ☆ The Crypt of the poets Adam Mickiewicz and Juliusz Słowacki.

The Crypt of Marshal Józef Piłsudski ☆ The Sigismund Bell, 1520.

In the nineteenth century Wawel began to function as a national pantheon, and this function has continued since. Among the royal tombs in the Cathedral crypts the tombs of national heroes appeared (Tadeusz Kościuszko, Prince Józef Poniatowski, Marshal Józef Piłsudski and General Władysław Sikorski) as well as great Romantic poets (Adam Mickiewicz and Juliusz Słowacki). Only occasionally major works were undertaken, such as the transformation of Bishop Padniewski's Chapel into the mausoleum of the Potocki family. Its elegant neo-Classical interior was designed by the Viennese architect Peter Nobile and completed in the years 1832–1840. Its altar contains *The Crucifixion* by the renowned seventeenth-century Italian painter, Francesco Guercino. The marble figures were carved after the designs by Berthel Thorvaldsen, who was one of the greatest sculptors of European neo-Classicism. Thorvaldsen also carved the memorial to Włodzimierz Potocki in the Holy Trinity Chapel. Some decorative works were carried in the Cathedral in the late nineteenth and early twentieth centuries, such as the wall-paintings by Włodzimierz Tetmajer in the Holy Trinity Chapel and those by Józef Mehoffer in the Szafraniec Chapel and in the Cathedral Treasury.

The thousand-years-old tradition of the Cracow see and Cathedral is represented not only by the architecture of the Cathedral and its monuments. The Cathedral Treasury is the unique, oldest Polish museum which has preserved, among other items, St. Maurice's spear, the memento of the meeting of King Boleslaus the Brave and the Emperor Otto III in 1000. The Chapter Archive, on the other hand, contains the richest Polish set of medieval documents. Some historical items relating to the Cathedral are accessible to the general public in the Cathedral Museum in one of the houses which once belonged to the Chapter.

A night view of Wawel Hill from the north-west.

Today, at the close of the twentieth century, Wawel Hill, which is visited every year by about three million people, functions primarily as the great historic complex of high artistic merit. For Poles, however, it means much more. The Castle is a living monument to the might of the old kings. The Cathedral is, like a thousand years ago, the first church of the vast see, the place where St. Stanislaus and St. Queen Jadwiga are worshipped, and the church where the great mission of Archbishop Karol Wojtyła – now Pope John Paul II – began. As in the Romantic period, Wawel is still a memorable national shrine where religion and nationalism are closely intertwined. Those who want to experience their visit to Wawel Hill in the full sense should keep in mind the unique functions of this unique place.

The sculpture of the Wawel Dragon, by Bronisław Chromy.